FOREWORD BY
Bishop Moses Owusu-Sekyere

PRAYING FROM A
PLACE OF AUTHORITY

Strategic Prayers

CHRISTA AFFUL

Copyright © 2023 by Christa Afful

All rights reserved. No portion of this book may be reproduced, stored in a retrieval system, or transmitted in any form or by any means – electronic, mechanical, photocopy, recording, scanning, or other – except for brief quotations in critical reviews or articles, without the prior written permission of the publisher.

ISBN: 978-1-916692-01-5

Cover/Layout Design
Bright Amoako-Attah

Editing
Mrs. Rita Agyei-Poku

CONTACT AUTHOR VIA
info@christaafulministries.com

Published in the United Kingdom by
EQUIP PUBLISHING HOUSE

This book is dedicated to all those who desire a sustained and fervent prayer life. My heartfelt prayer is that, as you engage with the pages of this book, you will truly encounter the presence of God.

Contents

Dedication	iii
Acknowledgements	vii
Foreword	ix
Introduction	x
Praise and Thanksgiving	1
Command Your Morning	7
Prayer to Walk in Purpose	13
Prayer for Uncommon Favour and Establishment	18
Prayer for Career and Open Doors	24
Prayer Against Failures	30
Prayer to be Debt-Free	36
Prayer for Wealth, Financial Breakthroughs, Opportunities, Divine Helpers, Strategies and Creativity	43
Prayer for Rulership Over Your Spirit	49
Prayer for Peace of Mind (Against Anxiety, Fears, Stress, Negative Voices)	55

Prayer for Wisdom, Counsel and Great Intellectual Abilities	61
Prayer for Divine Restoration	67
Relationships	73
Prayer Against Unforgiveness, Bitterness and Offences	79
Prayer for Healing	84
Prayer for Conflict Resolution	89
Engaging in Spiritual Warfare	95
Prayer for Your Community, Leaders and Nation	100
Prayer for the Nations	107
Salvation Prayer	113

Acknowledgements

I would like to express my heartfelt gratitude and appreciation to God and people who have supported me throughout this journey of writing and completing this book.

First and foremost, I want to give thanks to God for divine inspiration and ability to complete this book. I would like to acknowledge my loving husband, Justin. Your unwavering belief in me and your constant encouragement have been the driving force behind my perseverance. Your patience, understanding, and countless sacrifices have allowed me the time and space to pursue my passion for writing. Thank you for being my biggest cheerleader and always reminding me of my potential.

To my dear children, Jedidiah, Caleb, Jahdiel and Rochelle, words can not fully express how grateful I am for your presence in my life. Your boundless love, joy, and intelligence have brought light and inspiration to every step of this writing process. Your laughter and hugs have been my motivation during challenging times, reminding me of the importance of sharing my journey and insights with others.

I am also indebted to my parents, Kweku Bilson-Ekwam and Margaret Bilson-Ekwam, who have been pillars of support throughout this endeavour. Your belief in me and your words of encouragement have uplifted my spirits and provided me with the strength to persevere, even in the face of doubt or obstacles.

I will like to express my profound gratitude to Bishop Moses Owusu-Sekyere for ushering me into ministry and supporting me through this journey.

Additionally, I want to express my appreciation to my project manager, Apostle Douglas, and the publishing team who have believed in the potential of this book and have worked tirelessly to bring it to fruition. Your expertise, guidance, and unwavering commitment to excellence have been invaluable.

Finally, I would like to extend my gratitude to all the readers who have taken the time to explore the pages of this book. It is my sincerest hope that you find inspiration, guidance, and a deeper connection with God as you embark on your own prayer journey.

To each and every person who has played a part in the creation of this book, . whether through direct or indirect support, your presence in my life is cherished, and I am eternally grateful. Thanks, Dionne, for your immense support.

With heartfelt appreciation,
CHRISTA AFFUL

Foreword

In this book, Christa Afful has provided a comprehensive guide on the power of strategic prayers. As believers, we are called to pray without ceasing and to make our requests known to God. However, there is a need for us to understand the importance of strategic prayers.

Through personal experiences and biblical references, Christa has shown how strategic prayers can help us to align our thoughts and actions with God's will. She has also highlighted the different types of prayers that we can use to address specific needs in our lives and the lives of those around us.

This book is a valuable resource for anyone seeking to deepen their prayer life and to experience the power of God's intervention in their lives. I highly recommend it to anyone who desires to see God's will fulfilled in their lives and in the world around them.

May this book inspire and equip you to pray strategically and to experience the fullness of God's blessings in your life.

BISHOP MOSES OWUSU-SEKYERE
Presiding Bishop: Word of Faith Mission (WOFM)
& House of Faith (HOF)

Introduction

Is there anything you wish God would do for you right now? What request would you make if you could see God face-to-face? How would you express yourself if God were right beside you to listen to all you had to say?

Right now, imagine God is here with you (He has always been, though), what will you say to Him? You see, a lot of us pray to God abstractly. There has been a religion around our prayers that has often made it a mere confession without conviction. We say a lot of things with our lips but not with a deep-rooted conviction in our hearts that God can bring them to pass.

> *"O You Who hear prayer,*
> *to You all flesh will come."*
> PSALMS 65:2

Prayers are not just confessions; rather, they are expressions to God even when they are non-verbal, knowing fully well that He can hear us, and He is attentive to all our requests. Therefore, we pray until our joy is full.

Many Christians pray from a position of unbelief and lack the patience to tarry in prayer. Consequentially, they become oblivious to answered prayers. Bible admonishes us to have faith when we approach God in prayer, knowing that He is a rewarder of them that diligently seek Him. The emphasis here is that due diligence in prayer rewards.

To be able to experience results in your prayers you must always align with the Word of the Lord and have conviction in the ability of God. Through prayers, we allow God to reign and rule in every facet of our lives, including our community. We recognise His Sovereignty and express our trust in Him when we call upon Him. We don't just call upon Him in prayer only when we are in distress. It is expedient that we call on Him daily and regularly; thereby, recognising Him as our source in this life. Jesus exemplified this by seeking His father regularly and even secluding Himself occasionally from the crowd to seek God in prayer.

Strategic prayers are where you partner with God through His Word to accomplish His will and purposes in the earth realm. God has provided us with prayer strategies which will enable us see results when we stand to pray, be it intercessory or warfare prayers. In these last days, He is raising an army which will help fulfill His end-time assignment on the earth.

Prayers are not supposed to be bargaining chip where we ask God to fulfil our materialistic needs. Rather, it should be a time of fellowship with the Father, and to enquire of His will concerning us. We have been placed on earth to rule and take dominion; hence, it is expected of us to pray from a place of authority and victory.

Notwithstanding, prayers are means one can invite God into any matter of life that is beyond them. Whatever you cannot change yourself, you change it on your knees in prayer. When you pray, do not stop until you have received your answers. People rush out of prayers without receiving any answers to their prayers and they conclude that God didn't answer them. But that is not true.

Strategic prayers must be specific such as targeted to a particular situation. Strategic prayers involve aligning our hearts with God's word and His desires for our lives. They require faith, persistence and the willingness to submit our plans and desires to God's perfect will.

One may say that they have tarried in prayer, yet their prayers are unanswered. God always answers prayers. However, these answered prayers may manifest differently from our expectations. He also allows us to build our faith and trust whilst we wait. An example is when you pray for a business and God gives you the seed of an idea. Timing can also be a determining factor when it comes to answered prayers. Sometimes, some of our prayer requests are time specific and in His own time, He will make all things beautiful.

Lack of knowledge and understanding in strategic prayer have led to many people querying God's ability to answer their prayers. However, unbeknown to them, He is also waiting on them to take their places of authority and bring divine shift in their situations. There is always *how to* pray, *what to* pray for and words that command results. We are encouraged to refer to God's Word and promises as He will never go against His own Word; thus, compromising His credibility.

This prayer book is highly recommended as it enlightens you about the effectiveness of strategic prayers or praying from a place of authority. This book will help you pray in a way that you can get results and get God's hands to move on your behalf. It is a book designed purposely for those who trust God to see transformation in their lives and their nations through prayers.

Get set for an encounter that is about to change your life forever!

PRAISE AND THANKSGIVING

"And at midnight Paul and Silas prayed, and sang praises unto God: and the prisoners heard them. Suddenly there was such a violent earthquake that the foundations of the prison were shaken. At once all the prison doors flew open, and everyone's chains came loose."

ACT 16:25-26

The importance of praise and worship has been evidenced in the Bible and our daily Lives. It is stated that God inhabits the praises of His people. When we praise God, He shows forth His power and deliverance. God desires that we praise Him, even in the most difficult moments of our lives.

Most times, we praise God not for what He has done for us but for Who He is to us. Many people assume praises to be just about singing songs and hymns to God. But praise to God is beyond words, songs and the lifting up of our hands. Praise to God is primarily a function of knowledge and revelation of Who God is and who we are as His creation. It is identifying the nature, character and excellency of God.

Remember, praise facilitates access to God. (Psalm 100:4)

Now, if praise God for Who He is, then what is thanksgiving? Simply put, thanksgiving means to respond to Gods goodness and grace with gratitude. As opposed to what praise means, thanksgiving is a token of appreciation to God for what He has done: the blessings, protections, promotions and all the good things in life that God has done for you are the reasons you should give Him thanks.

What happens to giving thanks to God when you experience the opposite? For instance, what do you think about God when you lose a contract? What about the death of a loved one? How about times you don't get what you pray for?

Do you perceive God to be wicked during those difficult moments? Interestingly, those difficult situations are considered as most appropriate moments to praise God because, it depicts your recognition of God's character, and demonstrates your trust in His ability as a saviour, deliverer and restorer. When you know God for Who He is, praises flow from your heart to Him, even when the worst happens.

Dear friend, God is good at all times; hence, praise Him always. You must never base your praises on your situation. Learn to praise God even in the midst of the storm.

Interestingly, God is most moved in your direction when you praise Him in the worst life circumstances. The truth is that people are quick to forget Who God is when an ordeal befalls them. However, those who know the character and nature of God can attest that He is not the author of evil.

In conclusion, let gratitude become your lifestyle. When you are thoughtful, you will be grateful. I implore you to never forget what God has done for you. Praise Him and give Him thanks today.

- Thank you Lord for the life You have given me. Despite all that I have been through, You have remained faithful and good to me. My soul rejoices in You and my heart makes its boast in You. (Psalm 34:2).

- Abba Father, thank You for Your mercy and grace. As I continue in praises to You, let Your grace be multiplied to me.

- In the name of Jesus, I praise my way to victory. Songs of praise and thanksgiving will never depart from my household. I decree that through praises, I am victorious over every life's challenge.

- As God delivered Paul and Silas from prison through praises, I decree and declare my deliverances from every spiritual imprisonment in life. I receive freedom through praise in the name of Jesus (see Acts 16:24-25).

- Dear God, I may be hurting, lonely and depressed, but I still praise You because Your Word says, *"For in Death there is no remembrance of You; in the grave who will give You thanks?"* (Psalms 6:5). So long as I live, I will always praise You because I know you will give me victory in everything I go through in life.

- As I lift my voice in praise, I make a declaration that every obstacle or limitation in my life is giving way now, just like the wall of Jericho fell after the shout of hallelujah (see Joshua 6:20).

- I declare that my praise and thanksgiving are birthing divine multiplication in my finances, business and resources.

- I thank you Lord for bringing to nothingness the plans of the evil one against my life (see Psalms 21:11).

- My Jehovah Jireh, I honour You with lifted hands; for every good thing I possess has been by Your divine provision.

- Lord, I profess that I will forever sing of Your mercies, goodness, grace and loving-kindness in my life all my days.

- I decree and declare that my praise and thanksgiving are causing innumerable angels to locate me now with divine treasures.

Prophetic Declarations

- The LORD will surely comfort me and look upon me with compassion on all my ruins; He will make my deserts like Eden, my wastelands like the garden of the LORD. Joy, gladness, thanksgiving and the sound of singing will never leave my abode.

- The song of praise and thanksgiving will not cease from my lips. As I worship, my heaven is open for increase, multiplication and abundance of rain.

- Henceforth, the shout of joy and victory resounds in my home and the right hand of the Lord upholds me strongly.

- I declare my praise will become a sweet-smelling sacrifice unto God, bringing good melody to the heart of God. My thanksgiving will be like a pure incense unto God always.

- Praise to the Lord my Lord and Salvation, Who has made me walk triumphantly over my enemies. He has given me the garment of praise, the crown of beauty and filled my jar with the oil of gladness.

- Through praise, I declare that I receive a double blessing for every shame of my past.

- I declare that the Heavens open unto me whenever I raise my hands to worship and praise God. The Almighty God will ride powerfully on the wings of my praise and honour His words in my life.

- I declare that anxiety, fear and bitterness are subdued in Jesus name.

- God is so good that He withholds nothing good from those who love Him and are called by His name. Therefore, I decree God's goodness over all the days of my life.

- I decree and declare an overflow in every area of my life.

COMMAND YOUR MORNING

"Have you commanded the morning since your days began, and caused the dawn to know its place?"

JOB 38:12

What is the first thing you do when you wake up in the morning? How do you take control of your day? Have you commanded the morning since your day began?

What you do first when you wake up in the morning greatly affects your day. At the dawn of a new day, there are numerous opportunities to start afresh and another privilege to tap into God's blessing for that day. The Bible says, *"Blessed be the Lord, Who daily loads us with benefits…"* (Psalms 68:19). There are daily benefits for you and I in each day, and we must know how to access them by commanding our morning.

> *"Commit to the Lord whatever you do,
> and He will establish your plans."*
> **PROVERBS 16:3**

Commanding the morning is to set the pace for your day by starting the day with God in the place of prayers. There are specific prayers you can pray to take charge of your day and own it as yours. You are to possess every benefit and goodness God has loaded into each day. However, the best way to do this is to command the day when it is still budding.

Avoid being in a rush to get out of bed without getting on your knees first to fellowship with God. Once you get it right with God in the morning, the rest of your day will be right, regardless of what happens. Surely, you will end your day right when you begin with God.

Whatever begins with God ends in praise. If you want to retire to bed at night with joy, you must know how to start the day with God. The truth is, God wants to give you the scepter of authority to command each new day to your advantage. Rise up and speak words of life and hope. Have you commanded the morning since your day began?

Prayer Points

- Thank You Lord for the authority You have given to me to command my morning. I hereby declare open heavens upon my day. I decree that my day is blessed with opportunities.

- I speak by the authority conferred on me by Your Word and command all the elemental forces to correspond with my purpose and efforts. Everything I engage my hands and mind to do shall prosper.

- I take authority over every demonic manipulation and activities orchestrated in the womb of the day against my life, family and business. By reason of the authority in the name of Jesus, I declare the devil is under my feet and I silence his activities in and around my life in the name of Jesus. *"And the God of peace shall bruise Satan under your feet shortly…"* (Romans 16:20)

- I command the angels of the Lord to deliver to me all that the Lord has prepared for me today. Only good news is permitted to come to me today. I receive the ministration of angels whom God has designed to minister good news to the saints (Hebrews 1:14).

- In the name of Jesus, I declare that my life is hidden in Christ; hence, no calamity will come near my dwelling. I frustrate every plan and agenda of the enemy against my life.

- Father, as you bring to nothingness the counsel of Ahithophel, make every conspiracy of the enemy against my life become foolishness (2 Samuel 15:31-32)—may their counsel against my life today will not stand; neither will it manifest.

- **The Bible says,** "*The hand of Zerubbabel have laid the foundation of this temple; His hands shall also finish it*" **(Zechariah 4:9). Thus I declare that whatever I have planned out to do today shall be successful.**

- **In Jesus name, every monitoring spirit assigned by the pit of hell against my life today will not succeed.**

- **In the name of Jesus, I declare that everything in the universe aligns to work for my good today.**

- **I superimpose the will of the Lord upon my day. May my steps be rightly ordered by the Lord.**

- **I declare I shall be successful in all my endeavours. I declare the boundary lines will fall in pleasant places for me, and I will have a delightful inheritance. (Psalm 16:6)**

- **Let the echoing of trumpets sounding with good news be heard in my home today. Only good news will locate me this day.**

- **I command the mighty warrior angels of Heaven to disarm and overpower every principality, power and satanic force that will attempt to intercept or siphon my blessings this day.**

- **I cover my entire household, workplace, business, community, church, nation and all that concerns me with the protective covering and preserving blood of**

Jesus. I decree and declare that because of the seal of the blood of Jesus, we are exempted from every destruction programmed into our day.

Prophetic Declarations

- Indeed, it won't be long now; things are going to happen so fast. Everything will be happening at once—and everywhere I look will be blessings! Blessings like wine pouring off the mountains and hills.

- The Lord is my light and my salvation; I step out today with insight, knowing what to do and where to go. I refuse to walk in darkness.

- Today, I decree that the grace of God is distinguishing me from the multitude. I will be singled out for favour and honour.

- The words from my lips carry God's authority; so as I speak, I create possibilities all around my life. Nothing will be impossible for me as long as nothing is impossible for God.

- The name of the Lord is my shield and my protection; I find solace and perfect peace in the name of Jesus. My home is secured in Christ and in God.

- The Lord will bless the works of my hands and cause the labour of my work to prosper. I am blessed in the morning and the nighttime.

- I decree nothing dies in my hand. My business, career and work shall prosper.

- I declare I will be relevant at all times, and I will be astute in my dealings.

- The Lord is my sufficiency; no loss, no lack or limitation for me today in the name of Jesus.

- Surely, goodness and mercy shall follow me all the days of my life. As I step out today, the goodness of this day is mine.

- The sky over my head will not be sealed with brass; my heaven will open for me and I will operate under an open heaven from today.

- Just as Jesus grew in favour with God and men, I (mention your name) will enjoy the favour of God and men, starting from this moment forward.

- I decree victory over every trap and battle of the enemy today. The devil will no longer win over my family, business and career.

PRAYER TO WALK IN PURPOSE

"You are worthy, O Lord, to receive glory and honour and power; for You created all things, and by Your will, they exist and were created."

REVELATION 4:11

Nothing that God created exists without a purpose. God is not wasteful, and therefore would not have created anything without a reason or just to waste resources. God knows you and chose you for His will right before you were born. He told Jeremiah,

> *"Before I formed you in the womb, I knew you; Before you were born, I sanctified you; I ordained you a prophet to the nations."*
> JEREMIAH 1:5

God's purpose for you is His intention about you right before you were born. You are not an accident. It doesn't matter how your birth came to be; so long as you are here, God has a purpose for you.

However, many people miss out on God's plan and purpose for their lives because they choose to live without God. Come to think of it, how can a product tell its manufacturer what to make of it? It is impossible. The truth is, you cannot live a purpose outside God. Anything you do in life that seemingly looks successful without God is mere ambition. Ambition does not bring fulfilment; only purpose does.

Consequently, God wants you to come to Him so that He can show you His plans and purpose for your life. Stop trying to figure out life by yourself. This is what many people do that leads to frustration for them. The purpose is not trial and error. Your purpose is specific and can only be found in God.

Everything about you has already been written in God's Word. Therefore, I urge you to search it out for yourself. Know what God has said and is still saying concerning you. Follow the promptings and instructions of the Holy Spirit and never stop at anything to add excellence to what you do.

Prayer Points

- Dear Lord, the morning, afternoon and night phases of my life start with You (Colossians 1:16). Prove to me this day that You are the architect of my life. Let every plan and purpose You have for me come to pass.

- Father just as your word states that *You have a perfect plan for my life* (Jeremiah 29:11), I affirm that everything in my life will work in my favour according to Your plans for my life.

- Father, let me discover Your assignment and purpose for my life. May I not labour like a fool, jumping from place to place in search of what You have not given me (1 Corinthians 7:17).

- I know that my advancement to my next level requires a test of faith. I pray You grant unto me the grace to pass the entire test that would propel me to my next level in life (James 1:2-4).

- By divine authority I destroy every counterfeit purpose the devil has prepared for me to distract me from Your plans and purpose. I walk in the reality of what You have called me to do on earth.

- In the name of Jesus, I pull down every strange altar erected against me and my purpose in the name of Jesus (Matthew 15:13).

- I declare that my life is a source of gladness to my family and everyone around me. Let every event work together for my good. No situation will cause me to lose my identity in Christ.

- I receive the strength to commit myself to daily prayers and study to find out God's Word for my life in time. I receive the power and grace to wait on God in prayer always.

- Oh Lord! Just as You chose Bezalel and filled him with your Spirit and skill, ability and knowledge in all kinds of crafts, please anoint me also with the right skill set I need to walk in purpose (Exodus 31:1-5).

- I pray Lord that You help me discover my purpose and give me the courage and faith to take courageous steps in response to Your guidance.

Daily Declarations

- From today, I receive divine backing as I begin to work in God's purpose for my life. Clarity dawns as I engage, heightening my awareness of God's presence in every facet of my existence.

- The Spirit of God will keep expressing Himself in my life as light, giving clarity to every confusion and voidness in my heart.

- My mind is enabled by the Holy Spirit to make the right choices and decisions that pertain to my purpose in life and destiny.

- I believe in who God says I am. Therefore, I manifest the life of God effortlessly through my words, actions, profession and character.

- I declare that due to my covenant with the father by reason of the blood of Jesus, it is impossible for failure to cohabit in my life. I declare the manifestations of ease, peace and sure mercies of God in my life.

- I enjoy covenanted results from now on. Everything I receive will only be on the bill of grace. An end comes to struggles and fruitless efforts in my life.

- The preservation of my destiny will forever remain in God. As I stay more in God's presence, I enjoy divine insurance from the attack of the enemy.

- My destiny shall never be cut off.

- I decree and declare clarity and knowledge of what to do at every stage of life. I am not confused. Clarity about the future unfolds to me with time.

- The Presence of the Lord will be my covering and His glory will shine upon my life. I decree that my life will glorify God and I will always make Him proud of me.

PRAYER FOR UNCOMMON FAVOUR AND ESTABLISHMENT

"You will arise and have mercy on Zion, for the time to favour her, yes, the set time, has come."

PSALMS 102:13

There are things you have been working hard to get but haven't received yet. This is not to despise hard work but to show you that there are things only made possible by favour. If you have to buy everything with your sweat, then you lack favour. Don't you know that favour pays bills?

The truth is, it's hard to sum up favour in a single word. Favour is not luck. It is what Heaven does for any man, even when the man does not warrant it. Today, you need to engage Heaven to receive favour for your life.

Favour is God's gift to His children. If God chooses to favour a man, the world around him will undoubtedly become transformed in the wink of an eye. When you are in favour with God, people, even those who despise you, will be compelled to help you and support your life course.

Consequently, there are two faces to favour:

- Favour with God
- Favour with men

The Bible talks of how Jesus grew and had found favour with God and men (Luke 2:52). Also, we see in the Scriptures how Joseph found favour with men (Genesis 39:21). You can also look at the life of Daniel. The Bible says, *"Now God had brought Daniel into favour and tender love with the prince of the eunuchs" (Daniel 1:9). These were just a few people whom the Bible recorded that they found favour before God and men.*

Anyone can receive kindness from men, but it takes excellence to receive favour before God and men. There are men here on earth that are gatekeepers to the next level you seek. If these ones approve of your work, you can be sure nothing will limit you. Becoming a person of excellence would bring you into favour with these people. Strive to be the best at whatever is committed to your hands.

We understand that divine favour would allow a person achieve remarkable outcomes with minimal effort, but this does not undermine the place of diligence and excellence. You just have to strive for mastery.

Consequently, if you want to be a strong contender for a special favour, you need to position yourself wisely. When you live a righteous life, you attract the attention of God, and once He is pleased with your life, you will enjoy favour with both God and others. If God is on your side, you will prevail no matter who is against you. Seek God with all of your heart and soul and let your actions please Him because your time has come, and you are the next person in line for unusual favour!

Congratulations!

Prayer Points

- I pray Lord for unlimited resources, success and favour in the name of Jesus. May Your uncommon favour rest upon me and setablish the works of my hands. (Ephesians 3:16-20)

- Lord as You blessed Abraham such that generations after him are still reaping the dividend of this blessing (Genesis 15:1-2), I pray You Bless me and make me a blessing to others. Bless my business and prosper the works of my hands.

- Spirit of the living God, please direct me to know and identify the amazing things You have in store for me (John 16:13).

- Lord arise and favour me. Let the anointing for favour rest upon me and make me prosper exceedingly at everything I set my hands to do (Psalms 1:3).

- I ask oh Lord for Your blessings to be constant in my life. Let me enjoy the daily benefits You load for each day. May the blessing and the prosperity of this day be mine (Psalm 68:19).

- I pray that You direct my path to be at the right place and at the right moment.

- I pray for the release of the garment of uncommon favour upon my life in all my endeavours. May the hand of God be evidential in my life.

- In the name of Jesus, I decree that those who have rejected me will open doors of opportunities for me.

- I reject the spirit of failure in any area of my life. I decree success in my profession, in my marriage, in my business. Henceforth, I walk in the favour of the Lord (Psalms 90:17).

- In the name of Jesus, I command every doubting spirit that has become a stronghold in my life be broken right now.

- I declare that by reason of Gods favour, blessings will follow me everywhere I go.

- Father Lord, let the rain of Your mercy and grace fall on me.

Prophetic Declarations

- As the river flows effortlessly and never turns back, so will my progress be in life; forward ever and backward never. I command every struggle to cease from my life in the name of Jesus.

- I refuse to labour endlessly; my work will bring me plenty and my effort will never be in vain. I will stand strong like an army of 10,000.

- I declare favour has been released upon my life, family, business and ministry; I am blessed and highly favoured by the Lord and the shield of favour encamps around about me and my family.

- The rain of favour falls on my business and causes it to spring forth with plenty. Never again will lack be heard in my residence.

- I decree and declare that the windows of Heaven open upon my business and career; providential favour is what I enjoy going forward.

- I decree that men and women will begin to favour me everywhere I go. I am distinguished because I am anointed, honored and chosen to be favoured by God.

- I receive clarity on the opportunities that the Lord has made available for me and I become an answer to peoples' prayers because of God's favour upon me.

- The protecting favour of God is upon my life and family. Therefore, no evil or sickness is permitted to come near my dwelling.

- I decree an excellence spirit upon every work of my hands as I begin to enjoy increase in my job, business and work.

- I declare everything I touch begins to work for my favour and nothing I lay my hands on dies. The prosperity key of favour is mine.

PRAYER FOR CAREER AND OPEN DOORS

"Commit your works to the Lord, and your thoughts will be established."

PROVERBS 16:3

The way to the top is to keep climbing. Your career will only be possible if you know what opens the door. There is no workplace, organisation or institution which you desire to work in that can't be yours.

JOB INTERVIEWS

First, you need to understand what is required of you to gain access to those places. Big establishments don't just open their doors to anyone. You must have something they need and be able to defend it well. This is why getting certifications is important in your career. If you want to enjoy open doors in your career, see to it that you add to the certifications you already have.

More so, you must be able to defend what you know. In a job interview, what the interviewers seek to know is how your skills can solve problems. Interviews are the best way to market yourself. Do it excellently.

Time Management

One skill that can distinguish you from the crowd is your ability to manage time wisely. You must learn how to control the time you spend on certain activities. Give priority to what is important to your life and work and less priority to other things.

You need some measure of discipline and goal setting ability to know what time management entails. When you make your schedule, be disciplined enough to know that you must finish your work as scheduled.

Managerial Skills

As you find your footing in what God called you to do and begin to gain height and stature, you will get to a point where challenges become inevitable. For you to transition from this current stage of your life to the next, you will need to add to your skills.

The major skill you'll need for your career transition is management skills. This skill will test your leadership capacity and ability to make wise decisions in complex situations.

Challenges will come to test your tenacity and ability to handle what is coming for you at your next level.

This is why you see that when people get to a certain point in their career, they feel like they are stuck and can't move beyond a certain level. The problem is that there is a new devil for every new level.

You must build the spiritual capacity to handle the devil in the next stage of your life. It is not enough to have certifications. While gathering certifications is good for your career advancement, there are forces beyond certifications that would contend with you in that next level.

> *"Beloved, I pray that you may prosper in all things and be in health, just as your soul prospers."*
> 3 JOHN 2

You see, it is God's desire for you to prosper in your career. This is why He will create open doors for you even in the midst of challenges. As we can see in the Word, God finds pleasure in prospering us, making our business work and creating progress in our careers. Isn't that amazing?

As you continue in your pursuit in life, never forget God. Always remember Him and put Him ahead of whatever you do. Let God lead and guide your steps all the way and you will see Him creating opportunities you never expected.

Prayer Points

- I thank You Lord for what You are doing in my life currently. Thank You for Your provision of open doors in Christ Jesus.

- In the name of Jesus I command the gates to the nations to open wide unto me. Grant me access to nations of the world and make me globally relevant in my business, career and endeavours (Isaiah 26:2).

- I pray Lord that You strengthen my feet in my career and help me scale through challenging moments in my career. Connect me with destiny helpers who would lift me to my next level in my career.

- May Your power bring me into connectivity with the high and mighty in my field of work and beyond. Empower me to be able to serve kings/leaders with my gifts, skills and abilities. I pray and receive the oil of influence and elevation (1 samuel 2:8).

- Holy Spirit, inspire in me new ideas and insights for my career. Give me inspirations for new innovations in my field (Job 32:8).

- As I walk in diligence, may my steps be orchestrated to meet global leaders of influence in my field and beyond in Jesus name (Proverbs 22:29).

- By reason of my divine mandate I command doors of authority to open and grant me access to the corridors of power in my nation (Proverbs 19:6).

- I pray Lord that You open the doors of influence to me. Let my skills, talent and position create higher grounds of influence for me (Daniel 1:9).

- In the name of Jesus I declare that the gates to the nations are opened for kingdom advancement, and I am strategically positioned to make global impact. (2 Corinthians 2:12)

- Abba father grant me the wisdom, understanding and intelligence to build the right relationships for greater impact.

Prophetic Declarations

- I declare I will never be without assistance in all my endeavours. I decree I will always have the divine assistance in my career and business deals.

- I declare I am blessed with wisdom to know how to build relationships for a better career.

- My understanding is open to know what to do every time.

- I believe in God's Word for my life and every one of God's promises will come to pass.

- I decree productivity, progress and promotion always in my career. I will progress in my career/business with divine speed.

- I declare I shall prosper in all that I set my hands to do. Nothing dies in my hands.
- I decree the heavens over my career breaks open today. I receive good job opportunities and decree good connections and unmerited favour.
- Nothing will be impossible for me because I am in Christ and I can do all things through Christ.
- Everyone divinely positioned to help me secure my dream job will not rest until they fulfil God's promises in my life.
- I declare I will be very articulate and appear with confidence at my job interviews. Hence I decree successful interviews.

PRAYER AGAINST FAILURES

"For a righteous person falls seven times and rises again, but the wicked stumble in time of disaster."

PROVERBS 24:16

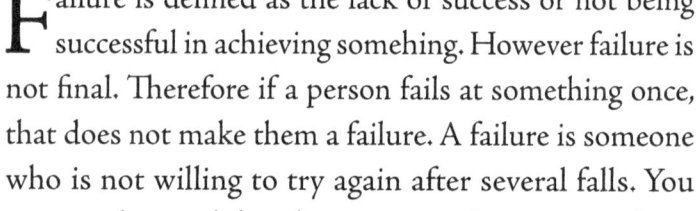

Failure is defined as the lack of success or not being successful in achieving somehing. However failure is not final. Therefore if a person fails at something once, that does not make them a failure. A failure is someone who is not willing to try again after several falls. You must understand that there is no age limit or time limit to trying again at something you believe you should be doing.

Never let naysayers talk you out of God's plan for your life. If there is a part of your life that seems not to align yet, never give up. You just have to learn through the process and try again.

Let me walk you through some of the ways to handle failure. This step-by-step guide works well with any aspect of your life that you think you are failing in.

Never Stop Trying

When you try once and it does not work, do not be quick to conclude that you are a failure. You must understand that nothing becomes successful without trials and errors. Recognising the positive aspects of failure is essential if you want to succeed in the long run.

Despite our mistakes, God wants us to grow from them. He is very concerned that we do not repeat the same errors. We must recognise our flaws and take personal responsibility for our acts if we are to improve. You can't fix an issue you won't acknowledge exists. However, you can turn your failure into victory, thanks to God's grace.

Sometimes we fail because we we were not able complete a given task due to our human limitations. However, you must not spend the rest of your life blaming yourself for failing at something you were never meant to do.

You Must Conquer the Fear of Failure

> *"For God has not given us a spirit of fear, but of power and of love and of a sound mind."*
> II TIMOTHY 1:7

Failure isn't the worst thing that could happen, but fear is. You can't move forward if you're paralysed by fear of the unknown. Anxiety and fear can stifle your creativity and create an internal struggle that is difficult to resolve. You'll never be able to do your job well if you can't think clearly. Resolve to succeed despite your fear of failing. Stride forward with tenacity rather than be skeptical about what you are about to do, if it will work or not. You must be bold enough to take the chance on what is important to your life and destiny.

Do What You Can and Accept What You Can't

It's common for people to believe they've failed when, in reality, they've simply failed to realise their limitations. You've been given a unique set of skills and talents to serve God. Do *something* for God even if you cannot do *everything*. Make a list of what you're good at and focus your efforts on that. Don't be obssessed with what you can't do.

Faith

You must trust that God is larger than your failure if you want to overcome self-condemnation. The ability to overcome failure is dependent on one's ability to maintain faith in one's own abilities. If we confess our sins to God, He is true and just to forgive us and purify us from all unrighteousness, according to the Apostle John (I John

1:9). God's character can be summed up in two words: faithful and just. Believe that God is faithful and just in His treatment of you. Keeping this in mind—God knows the end from the start. Learn to trust God and have faith in Him even in your toughest moments.

Lastly, your victory against the spirit of failure comes in the place of prayer. Now is the time to break free from the fear of failure and everything that comes with it.

Prayer Points

- God's expectation for me does not include failure (Jeremiah 29:11). Therefore, I will not fail in Jesus' name.
- Abba father, I commit my ways into Your hands. Please help me trust in You every step of the way.
- For God has not given me the spirit of fear, but of power, love and of a sound mind (2 Timothy 1:7), hence I reject and rebuke the spirit of fear from my life.
- In the name of Jesus, I receive victory over every failure of the past holding me down from making headway.
- In the name of Jesus, I pull down every stronghold of failure operating in my lineage.
- By divine authority I destroy every kind of spiritual barrier to my success in the name of Jesus.

- Through the power of prayer I destroy every limitation caused by fear operating against my progress in life.
- I claim my victory over the spirit of fear and failure in the name of Jesus.
- Father Lord, I rebuke depression as a result of failure in the name of Jesus.
- In Jesus name I neutralise any satanic attacks on my progress and renounce the spirit of failure.

Prophetic Declarations

- I renounce the spirit of failure by fire. Since Christ cannot fail, I will never fail. I am destined for success alone.
- By the fire of the Holy Ghost, I destroy every spirit of failure affecting my finances, family, business and progress in life.
- I declare I am carried on the wings of eagles; therefore, I receive double speed to run and outrun every failure.
- I decree and declare that every evil imagination and agenda cooked up by the devil to make me fail withers from the source right now.
- I decree that nothing will hold me back from fulfilling my destiny. I press on and become unstoppable. The works of God prosper in my hands greatly.

- I declare every hedge of limitation around me is broken and, like a bird, I escape from the snare of the fowler and break free from every hinderance to success.

- It will never happen that I will have a near-success story. The Lord has destined me to succeed and it will come to pass. I reject failure at the edge of breakthrough.

- Every attack against my mind is neutralised right now and the power sponsoring evil against my life to bring me down is destroyed right now.

- I receive the spirit of boldness to take bold steps towards my breakthrough and never to allow the discouragement from the pit of hell hold me back.

- Devil, take your hands off my life in the name of Jesus. Every enchanter, sorcerer and soothsayer behind my failing is humiliated and destroyed right now in Jesus' name.

- Every strongman assigned against me to make sure I fall to the ground, I decree that from today, such powers are rendered impotent.

PRAYER TO BE DEBT-FREE

> *"A certain woman of the wives of the sons of the prophets cried out to Elisha, saying, 'Your servant my husband is dead, and you know that your servant feared the Lord. And the creditor is coming to take my two sons to be his slaves.'"*
>
> 2 KINGS 4:1

There are many lessons, principles, and instructions about money and being debt-free in today's devotionals. Therefore, let your heart be open and get set to break free from the bondage of debt.

The truth is, nobody prays to be indebted. But what happens when you need money for certain things and are incapacitated? Or possibly you have an urgent transaction to make and there is no way around it? Maybe you have been trying to start a small business, and you need money to cater for some sort of business cost. How do you go about all these without borrowing?

Many people resolve to borrow when in need. While borrowing is not wrong, people borrow beyond their means and end up in debt. Debt is a serious issue that can cause ridicule to the debtor and destroy long-time relationships. When you need to borrow money to augment certain needs, make sure you don't become extravagant with it. It is unwise to borrow money to spend on parties, expensive food, clubbing and unnecessary outings or holidays. If you have to borrow at all, you should only borrow to invest in your business, add to your running capital and meet some emergency needs.

I have realised that people run into debt because they lack proper plans for their finances. There is no amount of money you can't plan for. Do not say you earn little, so you have to use everything for food. This is not a kingdom mindset. You need to create a budgeting system. Have a budget system that shows how you will divide your income based on percentages—food, housing, clothing, business or investment, savings and lots more. Proper budgeting will save you from unnecessary debt.

In planning, always save a certain percentage of your money for emergencies. Nobody prays for casualties, but they happen. So, the money reserved for emergencies will be used in some of these unprecedented circumstances so that you will not have to run helter-skelter looking for who you can borrow from.

Consequently, being debt-free requires discipline and many believers are not disciplined with money. If you want to be financially free, you must understand that buying should not be based on what you want but what you need. Stop being emotional about this; you don't have to buy everything you desire. Certain things can wait until later. Never allow anyone intimidate you into making you live above your income.

Lastly, you must understand that debt has no regard for anointing or office. A pastor can be indebted if he does not understand the principles of money. Look at the son of the prophet who died a debtor. That was definitely not God's plan for him. Yet, he died while indebted to his creditor.

Let all you learn today be part of your life and prayerfully trust God to help you get out of debt if you are already in it. I heard a story of a young lady for whom God used a helper to bring her out of a 3-year debt of $288,000 cumulatively. If God could do it for one, He can do it for all.

Trust Him!

Prayer Points

- Father, thank You for guiding me through these tough times. Though the economic situation around the world seems bad, I still enjoy Your provisions always.

- Lord empower me to make right financial choices and decisions. I have learnt that my current debt situation is consequential to bad financial choices. Grant me wisdom and strength to avoid repeating the cycle of debt.

- Holy spirit empower me to make wiser financial decisions. Teach me to know how to invest, what to invest in and right budgeting for my income.

- I implore you Lord to raise up helpers for me in the name of Jesus. Raise people for me who will help me get rid of my long term debt. Father, just as you used Elisha for the widow of one of the sons of the prophet, please use men to end lack in my family (2 Kings 4:1-7).

- In the name of Jesus, I refuse to be a slave to money. I decree money answers to me henceforth. I take dominion over my finances in the name of Jesus.

- By divine mandate I command any debt arrow shot from the pit of hell to be destroyed in Jesus name. (Isaiah 54:17)

- I affirm the word of the Lord and declare I am a lender and not a borrower. (Deuteronomy 28:12-13)

- Father Lord, break every curse of poverty over my family. I decree freedom from any form of curse in the name of Jesus (Galatians 3:13).

- I declare that my past, present and future now belong to God Almighty. Let every strongman of poverty be broken in my life. I enforce the word of the Lord and declare every financial Goliath is fallen in Jesus name. (Revelation 12:11)

- In the name of Jesus let every demonic mark be removed from my life. By virtue of the anointing let every yoke of slavery be destroyed and broken off my life.

- In the name of Jesus I announce the retirement of every spirit of debt that has been assigned by the enemy to make my life meaningless. I enforce the word of God and declare I am made for signs and wonders. As a child of God, I pray that You will come to take control of my entire being, and destroy any evil in my life that isn't supposed to be there, and allow me to live out my full potential in the name of Jesus (Isaiah 8:18).

- I cancel every inherited debt in my lineage in the name of Jesus.

- I pray for financial increase and abundance that will cause a sustained financial breakthrough.

- Oh Lord cause my financial cup to overflow. I receive the grace and anointing for good management and stewardship.

Prophetic Declarations

- I pronounce God's favour upon my life and call forth open doors of financial opportunity, progress, promotion, salary raise and increase in sales.

- I decree and declare that I will not have 'just enough'; rather, I will enjoy overflow of wealth and riches so much that I will become a source of blessing to people around me.

- Due to my obedience to tithing, I declare open heavens and declare that I shall continue to enjoy God's ceaseless blessings in my life.

- I will no longer borrow. I speak prophetically that I am above debt and money will never be my master.

- Every mountain of debt in my life, I command you to move. Debt is gone forever from me, never to come back.

- I receive help concerning every debt yet unpaid. My debts are miraculously settled by the help of God and I am free from debt.

- By reason of the blood I neutralise any spiritual or physical debt. I declare I am delivered from every curse of poverty as I step into financial breakthrough today. I am blessed today and forever.

- Wealth and riches are in my house and I enjoy increase more and more because God has given me the power to get wealth, and He has done so while adding no sorrow to it.

- I declare all my debt paid in Jesus' name. I operate under grace and wisdom regarding my finances.
- I decree that I am debt-free, justified and redeemed of the Lord.

PRAYER FOR WEALTH, FINANCIAL BREAKTHROUGHS, OPPORTUNITIES, DIVINE HELPERS, STRATEGIES AND CREATIVITY

> *"See, the Lord has called by name Bezalel the son of Uri, the son of Hur, of the tribe of Judah, and he has filled him with the Spirit of God, with skill, with intelligence, with knowledge, and with all craftsmanship, to devise artistic designs, to work in gold, silver, and bronze, to cut stones for setting, and to carve wood, for work in every skilled craft."*
>
> EXODUS 35:30-33

We are all born creative. It is God's intention that you should be able to transform what He has made and create something unique out of it. Our mind was given to us for a reason, and we must learn to use it effectively.

When you're creative, you're using your mind. The mind is God's gift to you; how you use it is your gift back to God. There is no limitation or impossibility with the mind. God designed the mind with the potential to replicate what He has created. In a way, your creativity reveals this part of your mind.

There is a part of your true self that wouldn't materialise unless you allow creativity through critical thinking. The most amazing part of humans is that God didn't make us robot; He created us in His image and His likeness. Invariably, we are like God. We have the ability to think (Isaiah 1:18) and make our thoughts reality. But how do you think and create without foreknowledge? You see, the raw material for critical thinking and creativity is knowledge. You are as creative as the knowledge you have gathered. Expose yourself to knowledge, ask questions.

The ability to think creatively is a great confidence booster. You become more resistant to outside influences when you have self-assurance. Challenge the status quo and see how you can achieve more with the power of your mind.

Do you know that creativity helps you become a problem solver and saves you from being part of the problem? Yes, the world needs creative people to solve the many problems we now battle day and night. Don't try to save your head by not letting your mind express its creative abilities. There are ideas buried inside you that can make our world a better place when you give such ideas wings to fly through your creativity.

Subsequently, only creative people recognise opportunities. A creative person will see opportunities where others see problems. This is why they always stand out from the crowd. You must have the creative attitude to recognise great people even while they are in their lowest states, divine helpers even when they do not look like it, and precious gold even when it is in its raw state.

Prayer Points

- In the name of Jesus I declare my heavens are open and the rain of abundance is released on all my endeavours. I declare my life has been endowed with heavenly blessings hence everything I find my hands doing shall be blessed (Deuteronomy 28:8–9).

- Father Lord, infuse my mind, body, and spirit with fresh ideas and creativity to become a problem solver. Inspire me to be creative and original like you are. Help me think outside the box.

- I confess that I lack nothing that pertains to life and godliness. Everything good that the Lord has prepared for me becomes mine this day. No lack. No loss. There are no limitations in my mind (2 Peter 1:3).

- Dear Lord please reveal to me the good works you have planned as I seek your face in prayer.

- I pray Father that You allow your imagination to spark my own imagination! Breathe Your life into me, and allow me walk in Your light.

- Grant me wisdom and intelligence in multiplying my financial ability. With the aid of the Holy spirit please guide me to know the right investment and right business location.

- May your Spirit enlighten me to several streams of income for financial prosperity (Psalm 145:16).

- Abba Father, increase my creativity to be more productive by Your Spirit, in the name of Jesus. Like Bezalel, the anointing for creativity rests upon me (Genesis 31:1-2).

- Open my mind to creative ideas that can make me wealthy. Grant me the exposure I need for new business ideas and creativity.

- In the name of Jesus, I set ablaze every evil power that put my finances in a cage. Right now, I decree freedom from poverty and lack.

Prophetic Declarations

- My mind is creative because I have the mind of Christ. My thoughts are pure and innovative because they are the thoughts of Christ. (1 Corinthians 2:16)

- I am happy and grateful because money flows in my direction in increasing quantities through multiple streams of income.

- Henceforth, I reject poverty and lack in my life. I declare that the covenant of increase and multiplication works in my life.

- I receive the right knowledge for prosperity—all that I need to know to walk in great wealth from now on.

- The power of God will cause doors of opportunity to open before me today. The mind of Christ in me makes me more creative as I receive divine ideas that would put an end to lack in my household starting today.

- My land will become more productive, and its yield will grow. I will have plenty and never lack anything good that pertains to life and godliness.

- I decree the breath of life from God upon my business. Everything I do with my hands is prospered by the breath of God. My business increases, and my barn bursts out with plenty.

- By the wisdom of God and my understanding, wealth flows in my direction. I have plenty of gold and resources in my treasure from today.

- Because the labour of a fool exhausts them all, I refuse to work like a fool. I know what to do and where to commit my resources, which would yield great results/outcomes for me.
- I do business under the inspiration of the Holy Spirit, as I receive the guidance and leadership of the Holy Spirit to operate in great wealth.
- I pray for the oil of favour to attract destiny helpers. May my business attract investors and people of influence in my business space. I reinforce the realignment of divine order to my life.

PRAYER FOR RULERSHIP OVER YOUR SPIRIT

"He who is slow to anger is better than the mighty, and he who rules his spirit than he who takes a city."

PROVERB 16:32

Now, the definition of mightiness is not physical strength but mental capacity. A mighty man or woman is not just a man or woman that can fight his/her enemy and win every battle like David, or the ability to lift the gates of cities like Samson. Mightiness has to be more than all these. Consider Gideon when God called him "the mighty man of valour" (Judges 6:12). Of course, Gideon had never won any war before that time. Why then was he called a mighty man?

SELF-CONTROL

A mighty person is known by the strength of their character. You can never be mightier than how you handle people and situations. Great people train themselves to overlook any situation that would trigger war, pain and chaos. You cannot be identified with greatness if your emotions still guide your actions. For instance, reacting to everything that makes you angry is not the way to greatness. Learn to hold your peace and observe the situation. You will need to discipline yourself to not allow anger rule over your life.

Anger

There are several places in the Bible where anger has brought people down. One of those people was Moses, a well-respected man in his dispensation and now. Moses did not enter the Promised Land because he disobeyed God out of anger with the Israelites (Numbers 20:10-11). God told Moses to speak to the rock, but he struck it twice in anger. Although God still made water come out, Moses' anger cost him the Promised Land.

Ability to Regulate Emotions

The truth is that prayer will not do what knowledge will do when handling emotions. First, you need to know what triggers your emotions. Identify these things and avoid them. It all takes discipline and self-control. Anger is like a disease; it will become an incurable disease that stays forever if not taken care of. Whatever controls you can rule over you when you allow it to continue.

Here is a piece of good news for everyone struggling with anger. When you get to the end of your rope, God becomes more willing to help you out. If you have been struggling with the issue of anger and lack of self-control, it is time to call on God.

Prayer Points

- I receive victory over the spirit of anger in me. In the name of Jesus I command every strange spirit of anger in operation in my life to make me lose what God is preparing for me is destroyed right now in the name of Jesus (II Timothy 1:7).

- I will not destroy God's plan for my life due to anger. All that the Lord has prepared for me will be mine tangibly and I refuse to let anger make me destroy God's work with my own hands (Exodus 32:19).

- I decree today that my emotions will not rule over my spirit. I walk in the spirit and in the light of God's Word. In the name of Jesus, my choices and decisions of destiny will never be emotionally engineered.

- I receive emotional intelligence and stability to know what to do and how to do it, irrespective of what is happening around me (Luke 12:22-23).

- Father please keep me under your wings and cover me under your shadow, away from any form of mental, physical or emotional damage (Psalms 91:1).

- Father Lord, heal my wounded heart. Please heal me of every pain I have suffered, the deep anguish I have gone through and the ordeal that I have passed through (Psalms 51:17).

- Father, You know everyone going through hard times. Please Lord, meet everyone at the very point of their need. Grant unto them support, strength, hope and life in Christ Jesus (John 7:38).

- I pray for divine refreshments to my weary heart. My soul feels sour and my heart heavy. Lord Jesus, help me find peace and comfort in You in the name of Jesus.

- As I meditate on your word, may it fill my heart and calm my nerves whenever the tension of anger builds up in me again.

- Father as I reflect on the characteristics of Christ, please grant me the ability to be calm and patient in all my doings.

- My Father and Lord, Your Word says, *"...no condemnation for those who are in Christ Jesus, because through Christ Jesus the law of the Spirit Who gives life has set [me] free"* (Romans 8:1, NIV). So, I agree with Your Word and decree that I am free from every form of shame and victimhood.

- I pray for emotional intelligence which will grant me the capacity to be aware of self control and the ability to handle interpersonal relationships judiciously. May my character reflect you.

- Whenever I feel hatred in my heart towards my neighbour, let your abundant love fill my heart in the name of Jesus.

- Lord Jesus, I pray that You will set me free from the shackles of slavery to resentment in the name of Jesus.

- I refuse to be frustrated; I refuse to harbour a feeling of inferiority among my peers in Jesus' name.

- Henceforth I will be intentional in being at peace with everyone in the mighty name of our Lord Jesus. Amen.

Prophetic Declarations

- In the Presence of God is the fullness of joy. Therefore, I declare joy overflowing. Nothing will steal my joy and no situation will make me cast away the joy of the Holy Ghost in my heart (Psalm 16:11).

- Christ has come to give me life in abundance, and I enjoy this life and experience all the goodness of the Lord for the rest of my life.

- The Prince of peace would cause His peace to spread over my heart and I enjoy absolute tranquility even in the most bizarre situations of life.

- Regardless of the pain and sorrow I have struggled in the past, today marks a new beginning of change for me. I operate under another covenant that brings peace, joy and love forever.

- Fear no longer has a grip on my heart because the Holy Ghost has already taken over my heart and made it His dwelling place.

- When my thought takes me down with the feeling of anxiety and impossibility, I look up to God for help. Help comes for me always when I am in my lowest state. I am not without help.

- The secret place of the Most High is my safety and I hide under the wings of the Almighty. I decree stability and perfection under the shadow of God's mighty hands.

- Henceforth, I receive divine help to be anxious for nothing or not be worried about my situation. As I present my request before God in prayers, thanksgiving and praise will fill my mouth to God.

- The powerful Word of God will be my comfort in times when I am discouraged and sad. As I open my Bible to study, the Word of God becomes real and more true to me.

- No matter what I go through in life, God's voice will be my only succor. I receive grace and enablement to recognise God's voice whenever He speaks.

PRAYER FOR PEACE OF MIND (AGAINST ANXIETY, FEARS, STRESS, NEGATIVE VOICES)

"For God has not given us a spirit of fear,
but of power and of love
and of a sound mind."

2 TIMOTHY 1:7

What is peace of mind? Does everyone have it? Why do you need peace of mind? The mind is so powerful that it has become a major target for the devil. Once the devil can get through a believer's mind, he is 90% close to destroying them. This is why you must never allow certain thoughts, ideologies or perceptions to dominate your mind. Live in the consciousness of what God has done for you through Christ Jesus and not what your current situation dictates.

What allowed Jesus to sleep on the boat despite the fearful tempest? (Mark 4:38-40). Of course, this is evidence of the peace of mind Jesus had. Having peace of mind means being unperturbed even in the face of challenges. God does not promise us a trouble-free life, but you must know that He has assured us of His Presence even amid the troubles.

Furthermore, you need to fight the devil in your mind to break out from his lies and deceits. The devil uses subtle trickery of negative suggestions to deceive the human mind. He suggests thoughts contrary to God's Word and creates a picture of fear in your heart. But remember, God has not given us the spirit of fear (2 Timothy 1:7).

Whenever a thought pattern produces fear and anxieties in your mind, be quick to refute it and counteract it with the Word of God. You can't win the devil's thought with your thoughts. You must win with your confessions.

God's Word comes to encourage, instruct, comfort and create faith in your heart. Any thought contrary to these is from the devil.

Prayer Points

- Lord Jesus, I thank you for a new day like this. You have blessed this day for me and I am grateful for each blessing you have loaded into the day for me (Psalms 69:19).

- Let every veil of fear and darkness cast over my mind be removed in the name of Jesus. I receive clarity, insight and direction today.

- I expose the wickedness of the wicked, those who are hiding in darkness to kill, cause havoc and spread fear. Let not their hands be able to perform their enterprise (Job 5:12).

- I speak peace over every storm in my life. May my marriage, business and profession receive the peace of God today. In the name of Jesus, I decree, "*Peace, be still*" (Matthew 8:23-27).

- I block any access the enemy would want to use to steal my joy, peace and strength. I pray for the grace guard my heart and mind against the enemy's devices. (Proverbs 4:23)

- I use my shield of faith to block every fiery darts of the enemy against my vision, mind and soul. (Ephesians 6:16)

- Dear Lord, although at times I get terrified after receiving frightening news, yet I will choose to trust you. Please, grant me the strength to weather the storm coming. Give me the courage to walk through it all knowing that You are always with me (Hebrews 13:5).

- The Word of the Lord says, "*O Death, where is* your sting? O Hades, where *is* your victory?" (1 Corinthians 15:55). Therefore, I break free from the grip of Death and bask in the resurrection power of Jesus Christ.

- As I stay intimate in prayer with you, may I become more like you in my deeds. Cause me to reflect your characteristics in my communication and lifestyle. Cause me to be established in faith, love, righteousness, peace and the joy of the Holy Ghost.

- I confess that your kingdom has come into my heart and whatever you have not planted in my heart be uprooted right now in Jesus name. (Matthew 15:13)

- I shut up every accusation of the devil against my life. Every lie of the devil fighting my peace of mind and causing anxiety for me is silenced in the name of Jesus (Hebrews 2:10-18).

- When I can't find my balance and my soul becomes disturbed like the turbulent sea, help me to know You are always with me.

- Father Lord, give me the clarity of mind to find Your purpose for my life and walk in it without fear of any kind.

Prophetic Declarations

- This nation and its inhabitants will not cause me trouble. I decree peace over this nation (Psalms 122:6) and enjoy God's peace all around my life.

- The Lord is the light of my life, whom shall I fear? The spirit of fear has no place in my life henceforth. I decree that the Lord will forever be my light (Psalms 27:1).

- *"He suffered no man to hurt them: and He reproved kings for their sakes. He did not allow anyone to oppress them, or any kings to reprove them"* (**Psalms 105:14**). Forever, this will be my testimony.

- Though the earth may rage and the people conspire evil, my heart will dwell safely in the love of God because the love of God is my solid hope and foundation.

- I enjoy peace of mind in every situation, strength when I am weak, hope when I am fainting and grace when I am helpless (Deuteronomy 31:6).

- I decree and declare that help comes to me from the four corners of the earth. Those who do not know me will hear of me and will want to help me. I am marvelously assisted by God (II Chronicles 26:15).

- The peace of God that surpasses human understanding fills my heart like a still river. Henceforth, nothing troubles my heart nor moves me to fear.

- I decree absolute calmness over every troubled water of my life. I say, "Peace, be still" (Mark 4:39).

- The devil will never have a way to access my mind and heart. The treasure of my heart is guided by the love of God and sealed by His words. No negativity is permitted in my heart.

- Jesus Christ rose from the grave so that I could live a victorious life evermore. I walk in this reality from now on. I walk in victory through Christ Jesus my Lord.

PRAYER FOR WISDOM, COUNSEL AND GREAT INTELLECTUAL ABILITIES

"If any of you lacks wisdom, let him ask of God, Who gives to all liberally and without reproach, and it will be given to him."

JAMES 1:5

The only way to make better decisions is through wise counsel. Many great men of old through wrong counsel, became mere men. On the other hand, people have built great empires through this wisdom. *"Through wisdom is a house built and by understanding it is established"* (Proverbs 24:3-4).

People have emerged from nothingness and have become mighty because of this wisdom. It is dangerous to be friends with an unwise person because foolishness will be seen in and around what you do.

The Bible says, *"He who walks with wise men will be wise, but a fools' companion will be destroyed"* (Proverbs 13:20).

Look at your life; do you have any wise friends? How do you distinguish a wise person from a fool? How can you become wise through association?

Now, wisdom is evident by the fruits it bears. You can know a wise friend by their lifestyle and the results you see around their life. Wise people work according to principles and are guided by a specific way of life. They are not emotional about their choices and decisions. They know what to do and go for it. A wise person will never compromise in order to have what others have. He knows what he wants and allows wisdom to direct him rightly. Observing the life of a wise friend can make you wise too.

Notwithstanding, there is another level of wisdom that does not come through books or by reading people's life; it comes by contact with the Spirit of wisdom. God is Spirit and He is the embodiment of wisdom. If you want to contact this wisdom, you need to contact God. Through Jesus Christ, we have been given access to the wisdom of God.

> *"The fear of the Lord is the beginning of wisdom: and the knowledge of the Holy One is understanding."*
> PROVERBS 9:10

The fear of God being the beginning of wisdom means there is more wisdom to be accessed. The more you quest after God, the greater the dimension of wisdom you will experience and manifest. You will be surprised at the height of intellectual capacity you will begin to operate in due to your relationship with God through prayers and His Word.

My last piece of advice for you on this topic is that you must never forget your source. Many have grown so much in wisdom that they assume they are what they are by their ability. A river that forgets its source will soon dry up. Always acknowledge the Giver of all wisdom and never let pride take you away from God.

Prayer Points

- Father Lord, help me to be disciplined so that I can follow through the instructions You give me through Your Word.

- Lord Jesus, bless me with divine wisdom for right living. Let my choices and decisions be a byproduct of Your wisdom. May I never step out to do anything that pertains to my destiny without an instruction from You (Isaiah 30:21).

- Lord, it is not always easy for me to know the direction to take but I trust Your Spirit to lead me. Please Lord, lead me to the open doors You have set before me (Revelation 3:8).

- Abba Father, give me the right wisdom [as a Father, mother, leader of small group, minister], to lead people according to Your wise counsel (II Chronicles 1:10).

- I pray and receive clear guidance about marital decisions, business decisions and career choice. Direct my path and show me the way to go in life. Help me not to wander away and waste my time on frivolities (Genesis 31:3).

- Whenever it looks like I am not sure of how to pray for wisdom, please give me the right utterance.

- Your Word says that the companions of fools will be destroyed. Help me, Lord, because I don't want to perish with fools. (Proverbs 13:20)

- Father, You are the light-giver. Please light my path. Guide my way and shine Your light on my path (Psalm 119:105).

- I enforce the word of the Lord which gives me the wisdom to deal with difficult people and situations. Help me know how to answer a fool according to his folly and when to keep quiet (Proverbs 26:4-5).

- I receive wisdom to identify and understand Your will for my life and walk in it accurately.

- In the name of Jesus I receive divine intellectual abilities to make the right choices and decisions.

Prophetic Declarations

- I am divinely guided by the wisdom of God through His Word and I make no mistakes about any issues regarding my life and destiny.

- Henceforth, my life becomes an evidence of divine leading. For every step I take, I hear a voice behind me telling me where to go or which way to turn.

- The wisdom of God is seen in my career, profession, business and ministry in the name of Jesus. I express divine wisdom effortlessly.

- My understanding is enlightened by wisdom to do what is good and right even when it seems uncomfortable.

- The Spirit of wisdom rests upon my life and I understand more than the aged because I keep God's Word close to my heart and obey all of His commands.

- I receive wisdom and directions every time I need help to take crucial life decisions and I am made wiser than my enemies for God's Word is ever before me.

- God's Word is a lamp to my feet and light to my path and I will never make wrong moves or decisions.

- I decree that my association will be a company of wise men and women who are led by God's Word and inspired by the Holy Spirit.

- I decree, Lord, that You water my life with Your Spirit and Your wisdom so that my words will be wise counsel and my actions will be guided by Your Spirit.

- I receive wisdom for every situation of life; I know what to say and what to do to handle any situation that comes my way.

- I refuse to allow pride or self-doubt take the wisdom of God away from me. As I walk in wisdom, I will never stumble.

PRAYER FOR DIVINE RESTORATION

"So, I will restore to you the years that the swarming locust has eaten, the crawling locust, the consuming locust, and the chewing locust, my great army which I sent among you. You shall eat in plenty and be satisfied, and praise the name of the Lord your God, who has dealt wondrously with you; and My people shall never be put to shame."

JOEL 2:25-26

Divine restoration is God's way of bringing back to you what was originally yours, which you lost either through ignorance or negligence. Interestingly, divine restorations could be in any area of your life, including your health, relationships, spiritual life, etc.

Whatever the devil has stolen from you, God can restore your losses in double-fold today. Don't lose heart. Don't lose faith. Keep trusting God.

However, there are certain keys to divine restoration which you must realise. As much as God wants to restore your losses to you, you also have a role to play. Here are things to do to enjoy divine restoration:

- *Self-realisation:* Your first step to restoration is knowing what you need in God. If you do not know you lack something, you will never know how to get it.

- *Acknowledgement:* You need to acknowledge the fact that you have lost something important to the devil, either through ignorance or negligence. At this point, you acknowledge your fault and get set for a change.

- *Brokenness:* God does not despise a broken and contrite spirit. Be sincere to God as much as you are to yourself. Be ready for a change. Let God know what you want and embrace any instruction He gives you. Sometimes, restoration comes with knowing what God is saying and taking appropriate actions.

- *Return to God:* When that prodigal son squandered all that his father gave him, he said to himself:

    > "I will arise and go to my father,
    > and will say to him, 'Father, I have
    > sinned against heaven and before you...'"
    > LUKE 15:8

- *Likewise, you can do as the prodigal son did; return to God.* God is your source, but disconnection from Him means lack, backwardness, frustration, and hunger. Return to God and acknowledge Him as your Father. God is always ready to welcome you back to His kingdom anytime, just like the prodigal son returned home to his father.

- *Give yourself to a life of prayer:* Nothing changes unless you pray. Consistently engage Heaven for mercy.

- *Everyone needs divine restoration.* When divine restoration occurs, great things happen. To experience divine restoration, you must consistently choose God above your situation.

Prayer Points

- Thank you Lord for divine restoration which is released upon my life this day.

- I pray for a double portion of blessings for all the pain and shame I have suffered over the years (Isaiah 61:7).

- Every person or circumstances that has taken from me what is rightfully mine, in the name of Jesus, I decree, let it be released to me right now (Amos 9:14).

- I declare according to the word of the Lord that whatever the enemy has stolen from me is restored in the name of Jesus. Devil! Get your hands off my business, family and relationships in the name of Jesus. (Deuteronomy 30:3-13)

- Every strong man withholding my blessing, breakthrough and progress in life, I bind and cast you right now in the name of Jesus (John 10:10).

- Faithful Father, I know you are faithful to Your Word. Your Word says, *"For I will restore health unto thee, and I will heal thee of thy wounds, saith the LORD; because they called thee an Outcast, saying, This is* **Zion***, whom no man seeketh after."* (Jeremiah 30:17). Please, restore my health and heal my family of every emotional hurt.

- I decree restoration in all I have lost in my marriage, business, relationship and life. For me, let it be like when Israel returned from the captivity of Zion (Psalms 126:1).

- I renounce every hopeless spirit clinging unto my destiny because of my failure. I bind every spirit of frustration, depression and disillusionment in the name of Jesus (Psalms 9:9).

- In the name of Jesus, I paralyse every activity of spiritual and physical parasite fighting against my life. I rebuke every devourer from my life (Malachi 3:10-12).

- My Father and Lord, I might have wasted some years in my past, but Your Word promises me that You will restore the years that the locust has eaten (Joel 2:25). Please Lord, restore my wasted years.

- O Lord of all grace, please cause me to abound in financial grace. Bring me into a relationship with people who will open financial opportunities for me (II Corinthians 9:8).

- I pray for restoration for my family. Please, Lord, bind my family together in love and unity. I pray that everyone will forgive one another and allow peace to reign in our home (Proverbs 11:29).

- I pray for the restoration of my lost glory, may every captivity be turned into freedom. I comannd flesh to be restored on dry boes and let my flesh come alive again.

Prophetic Declarations

- I affirm the Lord restores to me everything I have lost to the enemy due to carelessness or a nonchalant attitude. My lost glory, lost job, dying marriage, all is restored right now.

- For my pain, I receive double honour. I decree double restoration today and I enjoy plenty for the rest of my life.

- I declare that the breakdown and breakup I have suffered in the past is turned to double breakthrough and the failure of the past becomes success for me in the name of Jesus.

- The Lord is my healer and my restorer and this is why I declare that every terminal disease is terminated right now. I declare this sickness is not unto death. (John 11:4)

- The angel of death hovering around will not find my place to stay. I speak life, health, peace and godliness over my life and family.

- I speak and declare that every harassment on my destiny ends today. My life will no longer be an object of mockery and shame.

- The Glory of Christ is risen upon me and as I am in Christ, I bask in this glory always.

- Whatever is not found in Christ will never be found in me. I walk as the perfect representation of Christ everywhere I find myself.

- My health receives divine restoration; sickness will not tie me down anymore. My physical strength is restored; my mental strength is restored, and I receive restoration in every area of my life.

- I walk in dominion to prosper, create wealth and enjoy the goodness of God all the days of my life. From today, I operate in financial wisdom to make the right financial decisions.

- My breakdown will turn to double breakthrough, failure turns to double success for me and my lack turns to double abundance.

RELATIONSHIPS

"Anyone who wanders away from this teaching has no relationship with God. But anyone who remains in the teaching of Christ has a relationship with both the Father and the Son."

II JOHN 1:9 (NLT)

Do you desire a relationship with God beyond church attendance? How is your relationship with others? Do you know what a relationship truly entails?

The truth is, it takes two to build a relationship. God created us as social beings and made us all dependent on one another for knowledge, work and collaboration. Relationship is another divine provision for us to learn and grow. Most times, God puts the answer to the questions of your heart on the lips of others. Hence, you must not despise people.

Value every relationship you find yourself in, because relationships are God's first training ground for humanity. When you can learn to love the man you can see, loving God Whom you cannot see gets easier and His love grows bigger in your heart.

Interestingly, you cannot be in any form of relationship without communication and commitment. These two factors are the pillars upon which every solid relationship stands. There are certain relationships you have to fuel consistently with communication and one of them is your relationship with God.

Creating a personal devotional time beyond church activity enhances your intimacy with God. The truth is that God wants you to always approach Him so that He can speak to you. However, sin and the busyness of our generation have distanced us from a time of devotion to God. You need to make up your mind to have a fixed time and definite place created to fellowship with God alone.

God desires a father-child relationship with you. He doesn't want you to see Him as a far away God who is not familiar with our human needs. No! You can imagine God being a loving father. He came in the form of His creation through Jesus Christ to redeem humanity to Himself. Surely, God became man because of the love He has for humanity. Therefore, always see God as a loving father and not some strange and scary being.

To feel loved by God is to treasure the fact that Jesus loved you. Your relationship with God starts with knowing that He loves you. Therefore, you should demonstrate the love back by loving others. The Bible says, *"If someone says, 'I love God,' and hates his brother, he is a liar; for he who does not love his brother whom he has seen, how can he love God whom he has not seen?"* (1 John 4:20).

God values the way you treat others. He wants your relationship with people to be for comfort, encouragement, help and admonishment in the knowledge of God. Be intentional about every relationship, especially your relationship with God, because this is the source that strengthens every other relationship.

The Bible says, "How can you say you love God when you do not love your fellow men?" (Matthew 25:40). This implies that God will honour your relationship with Him when you honour other people around you, regardless of who they are.

Learn to have a healthy relationship with your colleagues at work, neighbours on the street, friends and family. These are the people you see often and you must see God in them. Respect their opinion. Speak to them politely. Do good to others around you because God Himself will see this act of goodness to others as unto Him.

In conclusion, treat people well. Be godly and be good.

Prayer Points

- In the name of Jesus, everything holding me back from building a consistent relationship with You is broken. I will build consistent prayer and study time so that I will be rooted and grounded in You (Romans 12:1-3).

- Holy Spirit, teach me and guide me in the way of the Lord. Let the Word of God dwell richly in my heart and let the truth of this Word renew my heart for goodness (Colossians 3:16).

- Lord, even though I walk in the valley of Shadow of Death, I know You are with me (Psalms 23:4). Help me, Lord, to always have the consciousness of Your Presence in my life.

- I reject every spirit of hatred, denying me to love others expressly. Please, Lord, let the love of Christ find expression in me to others in the way I deal and relate with them (Romans 12:9).

- Lord Jesus, I break off from every relationship that causes me to lose my relationship with You. Bring to me a covenant relationship like that of Jonathan and David (1 Samuel 18:1-3).

- Show me Your way, Lord. I pray that You teach me Your truth and help me walk with You the rest of my life. Let no money, material things or people derail me from a closer walk with You (Psalms 25:4-5).

- Even in difficult times, I pray You teach my heart to trust You and rest in your unfailing arms.

- Father Lord, bring me into relationships that would be the bridge to my next dimension. I pray, Lord, that You connect me to my destiny helpers who will choose not to rest untill they see me succeed.

- I pray that I grow into the highest version of who you have created me to be.

Prophetic Declarations

- From this moment forward, I enjoy the fullness of God in my heart always and walk in deeper intimacy with Him like never before.

- I confess that the Lord will order my steps into covenanted relationships with friends and people who will love me and be willing to sacrifice for me.

- The love of God will be evident in and around me. Surely, God's goodness, love, compassion and tender mercy will find expression in me.

- As I desire God's presence daily, I decree that He will fill my heart with His love and cause my ears to pay attention to divine instructions needed for my life and destiny.

- Nothing will separate me from the love of God, even as I go about my daily activities, I walk and work in the consciousness of God's Presence around me.

- The power of God can raise a person and make him or her a place of refuge for people. I speak prophetically that the Lord will make me a place of refuge, comfort and safety for my family and friends.

- The price that Christ paid to restore me to God will never be in vain. Every broken relationship is repaired and restored permanently.

- As I wait on God, my heart gravitates towards His Word and I live to fulfil all of His commands by grace. I no longer let sin dwell in me or take me from a consistent fellowship with my Father.

- In the name of Jesus, I receive fresh grace for daily communion with God as He sees to it that no day passes by without my voice getting to the Heavens.

- I declare that nothing shall break my relationship and love for God. Henceforth, I will become steadfast in my faith journey.

PRAYER AGAINST UNFORGIVENESS, BITTERNESS AND OFFENCES

"Get rid of all bitterness, rage, anger, harsh words, and slander, as well as all types of evil behaviour. Instead, be kind to each other, tenderhearted, forgiving one another, just as God through Christ Jesus has forgiven you."

EPHESIANS 4:31-32 (NLT)

Bitterness, hatred and unforgiveness damage many people's health and well-being, causing them to suffer physical and mental harm. You are not safe from the torturers if you don't forgive others, according to Matthew 18:23-35 (AMPC). When it comes to this subject, I'm sure you can attest to the truth of what I'm stating.

Who do you think benefits the most when you forgive the person who hurt you? Of course, you are the one. I've always thought forgiving those who have mistreated me was really difficult. Alas! It was not so. Forgiveness is not just for the other person but for you to be free of the burden, pain and toxicity that come with bitterness against those who hurt you.

When I choose to forgive, I know that it is to my advantage in the long run. Forgiveness makes me happier and healthier. Also, by releasing the other person in forgiveness, you allow God to do what He does best—forgive you. According to Mark 11:22-26, our faith is hampered when we harbour grudges against others. If we don't forgive others, we won't be able to receive forgiveness from the Father. It's all about what you put in and what you get out. Sow mercy, and you'll reap mercy; sow judgment, and you'll reap judgment.

Furthermore, having a close relationship with God makes forgiveness easier. The adversary, Satan, cannot gain an advantage over you if you forgive others (2 Corinthians 2:10-11). The Bible advises us not to let the sun go down on our anger (Ephesians 4:26). The devil can't build a stronghold until he first gets a foothold. Don't make it easy for the devil to torment you. Forgiveness is easy.

If you wait until you're in the right frame of mind to extend forgiveness, you'll never be able to do so. Rather than giving in to the devil's temptations, choose to obey God and stand firm against the devil's attack on your mind. Indeed, God will heal your emotional wounds in due time if you make a quality decision to forgive (see Matthew 6:12-14).

If you're angry with God because your life didn't go the way you expected, you need to forgive Him. God's justice is unfailing. Despite your confusion, God cares about you, and it's a grave error for anyone to ignore the only person Who can assist them—God.

Prayer Points

- Dear Lord, thank You for being a loving and caring God. Thank You for forgiving me of all my sins and blotting out my transgression.

- Help me to always remember that forgiveness is for me and not for those who hurt me. Let me forgive as You have forgiven me too (Matthew 6:12).

- Although sometimes I feel hurt, pained and betrayed. Please heal me of every hurt that people have caused me in the past.

- Father I pray for supernatural healing of wounds caused by abuse, heartbreak and breakup, which are still standing as barriers against my prayers.

- Empower me to resist sinning against You in my moments of anger or distress.

- Lord Jesus, I ask that You grant me the ability to forgive those who offend me and never hold it against them.

- Dear Lord, sometimes I dont feel safe around the people who once hurt me. Please protect me when I am in their company.

- Lord I commit into your hands my broken pieces and pray for divine healing.

- Oh, my Comforter, please have Your way in my heart. Comfort me, Holy Spirit.

- Dear Lord, help me to learn how to forgive myself, knowing fully well that You have already forgiven me.

💬 Prophetic Declarations

- I decree and declare deliverance from bitterness, offence, anger and any form of resentment I have against people. I declare my heart is positioned to love only and never to harbour bitterness

- I receive divine enablement to walk in love always. The love of Christ is shared abroad in my heart by the Holy Ghost and I freely express it to others.

- I forgive and erase from my heart and choose to never hold grudges against people whom Jesus loves and died for.

- The Spirit of the Lord is strengthening me from the inside out so that I can find it easy to forgive people and help them become better.

- I am healed from every hurt from my past and pain that had kept me bound for many years.

- I prophetically decree that anger will no longer rule over my spirit because I carry in me a new Spirit—the Holy Ghost, Who teaches me all things.
- I declare I will view others as God views them.
- I refuse to allow the devil take advantage of me and entrap me in his snare of offence and unforgiveness. From my heart, I forgive freely.
- I hereby declare my liberty from bondage of bitterness and offences. I hold nothing against anyone. I only love them.
- From today, I communicate love to the unlovable through my words, deeds and actions. Everything I do henceforth will reflect Christ.

PRAYER FOR HEALING

*"Beloved, I pray that you may prosper
in all things and be in health,
just as your soul prospers."*

3 JOHN 2

Do you know that God made promises to us concerning our health? Have you ever found out what God says about your health? Is sickness God's desire for us? Searching through the scriptures, we realise that God's intention for us is perfect health. He desires that we live without sickness or pain. God wants you to live in good health and sound mind.

At creation, God's original plan was a world without sickness but by sin, through the fall of Adam, sin, death, and sickness came to humanity. From this point, the devil began to torment people with sicknesses and demons inflicted people with sicknesses. Because of the fall, all men began to suffer from one disease, sickness, or the other. Many do not even believe in perfect health anymore, but a man came and took away all our sins and pains—the man Jesus.

> *"Therefore, just as through one man sin entered the world, and Death through sin, and thus Death spread to all men because all sinned. For if by the one man's offense many died, much more the grace of God and the gift by the grace of the one Man, Jesus Christ, abounded to many."*
> ROMANS 5:12, 15

The death and resurrection of Jesus has brought us life in abundance. It has taken away the siege of death and sickness amongst us. It has given us freedom from them all. By faith in what Jesus has done, we can now live without sickness or pain. Through Jesus, we are delivered of every oppression of demons and are free from the devil's bondage. Therefore, we do not live under the fear of sickness anymore but in the victory of what God has done through Jesus Christ.

Your body is the temple of God. Therefore, sickness cannot dwell there. Stand on God's promises concerning your health today. You are victorious.

Prayer Points

- Lord Jesus, You have promised that healing is the children's bread. Today, I ask You, Lord, to heal my body. I am your child Lord; no sickness is permitted in my body in the name of Jesus (Mark 7:27).

- Thank You Jesus for healing me. You alone have borne my sins and my curses and have purged every sickness in my life through the gushing blood from your stripes, in Jesus' name (1 Peter 2:24).

- By reason of the blood of Jesus, I beseech You to heal me. Revive and repair every damaged cell in my body (Jeremiah 17:14).

- I affirm Your word which states, "Behold, I will bring it health and cure, and I will cure them, and will reveal unto them the abundance of peace and truth (Jeremiah 33:6).

- By the authority in the name of Jesus, and by the fire of the Holy Ghost, I destroy and uproot every form of sickness in my body now. Sickness, loose your hold on my life now! (Matthew 10:1).

- O, Lord Jesus, heal me for You are my strength. Restore my health for You are my helper. Take the agony of sickness far away from my life, in the name of Jesus. Amen (Isaiah 41.10).

- Father, I decree total healing in my body, spirit, and soul. Let there be total revival and restoration in my body no matter what has been damaged (Mark 10:27).

- By the Word of God, and the blood of the everlasting covenant, I decree total deliverance and recovery from every symptom of sickness. Let everything I have lost to the enemy—health, job, money—be restored double in Jesus' name (Obadiah 1:17).

- In the name of Jesus, I command the destruction of every arrow sent into my body by the enemy. My bones, veins, tissues and all other organs receive health now in the name of Jesus (Psalms 103:2-4).

- In the name of Jesus, flush out every disease and infection jamming up my body. Let the sickness that flies in the air never touch my dwelling or my family members (Deuteronomy 7:15).

- I pray let every organ, system in my body that is not working in its rightful order begin to respond to healing in Jesus name.

Prophetic Declarations

- I declare I live in good health and have a sound mind.
- I receive the wisdom of the Lord to walk in perfect health.
- I declare my body will never harbour sickness again.
- I access divine healing as a child of God.

- From henceforth I choose to walk in power and the knowledge of the word of God.
- I decree and declare healing and prosperity to my soul.
- I make a declaration that I will not be a victim of evil circumstances.
- I access all the blessings made available to me in the word of the Lord.
- I decree that i am in perfect health both in my soul and physical body.

PRAYER FOR CONFLICT RESOLUTION

"If it is possible, as much as depends on you, live peaceably with all men."

ROMANS 12:18

Christians must have effective biblical conflict resolution strategies whenever there is a problem. Conflict resolution needs to be practiced by everyone since conflict cannot be left unresolved. Of course, it is unavoidable, but it can be resolved amicably.

Conflicts have to be handled for relationships, work environments, and communities to enjoy peace once again. If confrontations are left unresolved, it will damage relationships and bitterness will begin to set in. God wants us to resolve problems. Biblical dispute resolution is shown to us in several ways in the Bible.

If disagreement arises, believers need to do their best to ease the situation. If the transgression is trivial or not too detrimental, the Bible urges us to overlook the offence (Proverbs 19:11).

Now, if someone offends you, you need to forgive the person and not keep it against the individual. For this method of conflict resolution, you would overlook the tiny transgression and never bring up the issue again. This kind of dispute resolution is biblical. Nevertheless, it should only be utilised for minimal hurtful offences.

Major conflicts need to be resolved from a different perspective. The Bible gives us knowledge for healthy conflict resolution for more difficult, destructive, or costly disagreements. For disputes like these, we are not encouraged to ignore the crimes but rather tackle them head-on.

To put things right, you need to address the person who hurt you. It's not about proving who's right or wrong when resolving a disagreement. Ultimately, biblical dispute resolution aims to rebuild the relationship between the individuals involved.

The goal is for the offender to be brought to repentance by the Holy Spirit, confess their sins, and make amends with the other party. Jesus urges us to treat the person who does not agree to these kinds of conflict resolution as "a pagan or tax collector" (Matthew 18:17).

The individual should be forgiven and their relationship restored if they return in time and ask for forgiveness.

Holding resentment or hatred toward others is not a good or intelligent thing to do. We are commanded to love one another and forgive one another, just as God has done for us (1 Peter 4:8; Ephesians 4:32).

For the sake of biblical conflict resolution, we must conduct ourselves in a manner of kindness, empathy and love. There should be no hostility, rage, or pride in conflict resolutions. The goal of biblical conflict resolution is to bring peace back into the relationship.

Instead of blaming others for our problems, we should look for solutions inside our own circles of friends and family. When a problem emerges, we should try our best to address it swiftly and with a heart of humility, compassion, and love, even though we shouldn't purposefully seek conflict.

- Thank You Lord for showing me the importance of conflict resolution from Your Word.

- I pray you help me to live in peace with everyone. Let my daily conversation be one that will restore peace and not cause violence, in the name of Jesus.

- Lord Jesus, enable my heart to forgive those who offend me. Give me a forgiving spirit which holds nothing against anyone. Let Your love be spread abroad in my heart by the Holy Ghost (Romans 5:5).

- Holy Spirit, please create in me a clean heart. Take away every heart of stone and weight that has kept me away from You. Teach me to love others as You have loved me (John 15:12-13).

- I choose to forgive and forget what my offenders do to me. I refuse to bear grudges in my heart. Let Your love flow ceaselessly from within me and even among my family. Teach us to love one another in truth and in deed (Matthew 6:12).

- I refuse to allow anger and bitterness to dwell in my heart in the name of Jesus. My heart is free from hurt and pain from the past.

- Grant me the patience to be silent when angry so that I will not use hurtful words on people. Let the words I speak be seasoned with grace and love (Colossians 4:6).

- Holy Spirit teach me to forgive and resolve conflicts fast. Let no grievance be heard around my home. Help my family to live in the unity of faith and help us seek peace with all men (Hebrews 12:14).

- Lord Jesus, please restore Your peace within my home, family and nation at large. You are the Prince of peace, please come and reign supreme in our nation and put an end to the mayhem the devil has been causing (Colossians 3:15).

- I pray Lord You allow love to reign in our hearts. Make us instruments of Your peace, where there is hatred, let Your love be seen in and through us in the name of Jesus.

Prophetic Declarations

- I refuse to be defined by anger, bitterness and hatred. My identity remains in Christ and as anger and bitterness cannot be found in Christ, they will not be found in me.

- I receive empowerment to forgive those who offend me and to love them just the same way Christ loved us all even when we do not deserve it.

- I receive help from the Holy Ghost to guard my heart against offences and bitterness of any kind.

- I speak peace to every troubled heart and declare, "Peace, be still." The peace of the Lord that surpasses human understanding fills my heart and every troubled heart around me.

- I decree that love leads everywhere. The love of God will find expression in my home, work, business and everywhere I find myself.

- I confront every spirit of strife, envy, bitterness and anger. Leave the heart of people right now!

- Henceforth, I practice restraint when angry. I will no longer let the spirit of anger rule over my life.

- From henceforth I declare the love of God is evidential in my speech and conduct. And because I am an embodiment of Christ His characteristics will be unveiled through me.

- I declare that Christ would be revealed through me to people through living peaceably with all men.
- I decree there will be no carry-over of issues or bitterness against anyone. My heart is full of love, kindness and goodness.

ENGAGING IN SPIRITUAL WARFARE

*"For we do not wrestle against flesh and blood,
but against principalities, against powers,
against the rulers of] the darkness of this age,
against spiritual hosts of wickedness
in the heavenly places."*

EPHESIANS 6:12

Do you desire everything God has for you on earth, or do you want to wait until you get to Heaven to enjoy victory and blessings? Of course, you will prefer the former. Through this prayer journal, you will understand why and how to engage in spiritual warfare to enjoy what God has for you on earth and reign with Him also in Heaven.

We are at war. From the beginning of time, spiritual warfare has been a contention between two kingdoms. The kingdom of darkness, which is ruled by the devil, is always at loggerheads with the kingdom of our God.

Right from when Satan fell from Heaven, he and his demons have never stopped warring against God and His creation (Revelation 12:7-17). We are waging spiritual warfare. To win this war, you need a higher spiritual authority. Why do we even want to engage in spiritual warfare? You see, we must question ourselves, or it will be pointless to talk about warfare or the purpose of fighting. We are either winners or losers. Jesus said,

> *"All authority has been given to Me in heaven and on earth."* MATTHEW 28:18

Awesome!

This same authority has been given to us in the name of Jesus. By the name of Jesus, we are not only saved but also empowered by God for victory over the devil's works. Your everyday victory is achieved by knowing, believing and understanding that the battle has been won even before the fight began. Hence, we war from a victor's perspective and not a victim's.

As Christians, it is not enough to just receive the life of Christ and decide you are now saved and severed from this war. No! The devil still tries to contend with even your salvation. Salvation is not the end of warfare against the devil. If it were, God should have taken you to Heaven when you were saved.

However, you are here because you have been enlisted into the army of Christ to fight for victory. It is time to consistently engage the weapons of prayers and the Word to keep an edge over the devil; *For the weapons of our warfare are not carnal but mighty through God through the pulling down of strongholds.* (2 Corinthians 10:4)

In a war, those who become victims are mostly children. This is because they are immature to handle what is going on in a war.

"Dear believer, it's time to transcend immaturity. Avoid engaging in a victim mentality during this battle. Engage in fervent prayer and wield the Word wisely. Your triumph resides in your words, so keep proclaiming it without ceasing."

Prayer Points

- I thank You Jesus for the power and authority you have given me in the name of Jesus to trample over every demonic activity (Luke 10:19).

- Oh Lord, baptise me with a fresh unction for prayers.

- In the name of Jesus, I destroy every strategy of the enemy against my life and family. I decree and declare that the plan of the enemy will not stand; neither will it come to pass. (Isaiah 54:17)

- By the power of prayer and faith in my heart I confess I will no longer worry or complain but rather focus on what You have accomplished for me in Christ Jesus. In Christ alone, I have my victory.

- As I lift my shield of faith I block every firey darts access to my mind and heart in Jesus name. (1 Peter 5:8)
- I rebuke and block every form of demonic activity around my life, family, relationship, business and career. I decree and declare, Satan, take your hands off my family, finances, and health.
- I pray let every broken hedge of protection be restored. I declare my gates are free from satanic attacks. (Ecclesiastes 10:8)
- By reason of the blood I neutralise and break every generation curses from my lineage. I decree when it comes to me and my children we are exempted.
- Anointing for uncommon favour fall on me now in Jesus name, and cause me to accomplish great achievements.
- I block any access the enemy has to my life. I pray Lord that You uncover my blindspots.
- Oh Lord, just as mountains surround Jerusalem roundabout, let Your fire surround me and shield me from the enemy's attack.

Prophetic Declarations

- I destroy every form of demonic operation set against my finances and I speak that their plans will not stand neither shall they come to pass.

- I command every form of disease-causing demon against my health to be totally abolished.

- Every dark force causing pain and destruction around my life is destroyed right now. No darkness is permitted in or around my life.

- I decree that every negative word uttered in the spiritual realm impregnated with evil intents against my life and destiny is destroyed. No enchantment or incantation against me will stand.

- I terminate any demonic activities around my families, homes, businesses and communities. I destroy their works and render them powerless.

- By the authority in the name of Jesus, I command the enemy to take his hands off my family. I declare my family is covered by the blood.

- I decree and declare that my inner man receives the fire of the Holy Ghost to fight and war against demonic activities in these times and seasons.

- I take authority over familiar spirits attempting to repeat the cycle of poverty, sickness and pain in my life. I stop demonic cycles right now in the name of Jesus.

- I nullify the activities of every spirit of death hovering around my family in the name of Jesus.

- I declare my family belongs to the Lord hence devil you have lost this battle over my life, family, children and business.

PRAYER FOR YOUR COMMUNITY, LEADERS AND NATION

*"Therefore I exhort first of all that
supplications, prayers, intercessions,
and giving of thanks be made for all men,
for kings and all who are in authority,
that we may lead a quiet and peaceable life
in all godliness and reverence."*

I TIMOTHY 2:1-2

Praying for "peaceful and tranquil lives in all godliness and holiness" is what we are instructed to do. What exactly does this mean? The most important thing is to pray for our leaders, not criticise them.

Leading is one of the hardest things to do, especially among people with different beliefs, desires, cultures and responses to situations. In leadership, you will need to create a thriving environment for all these people in a safe space. It requires creating systems that work. If the last few years have taught us anything, it's that leading or governing a nation in this new era requires different strategies whether facing social-economic issues or global pandemic. The Bible therefore encourages us to pray for our leaders to be successful and to receive the grace to govern according to God's will for His people.

In the Bible, the importance of praying for fathers to be good leaders at home is emphasised in various passages. These passages also highlight the role of fathers as spiritual leaders and the ones who provide for their families. One such passage is Ephesians 6:4, which says, "Fathers, do not provoke your children to anger, but bring them up in the discipline and instruction of the Lord." This underscores the responsibility of fathers as leaders of their families. They are to lead in ways that promote love, discipline, and spiritual growth.

Additionally, a passage like Proverbs 22:6 says, *"Train up a child in the way he should go; even when he is old, he will not depart from it,"* stress the importance of fathers' guidance in shaping the moral and spiritual development of their children. When we pray for fathers to be good leaders at home, we are indirectly seeking God's guidance for them to help these fathers fulfil their God-given role and create a nurturing and spiritually healthy environment for their families.

Pastors are spiritual leaders who guide and shepherd the congregation. They too are fathers. Praying for them helps provide the spiritual empowerment they need to provide sound teaching, guidance, and inspiration, and to ensure the spiritual growth of the community.

Just as fathers and leaders face challenges, pastors encounter spiritual, emotional, and physical difficulties. It behooves us to pray for our pastors and ask for God's protection, strength, and wisdom to help them navigate these challenges effectively.

Praying for pastors fosters their personal spiritual growth and relationship with God. A pastor's strong connection with God positively influences his or her ability to lead and serve the congregation.

The Bible encourages us to pray for leaders, as seen in passages like 1 Timothy 2:1-2: *"First of all, then, I urge that supplications, prayers, intercessions, and thanksgivings be made for all people, for kings and all who are in high positions, that we may lead a peaceful and quiet life, godly and dignified in every way."* This extends to praying for spiritual leaders, including pastors, as they guide and shepherd God's people.

Bible encourages us to pray for our nations for in its peace and prosperity we would prosper. For instance if a leader is into self gain and focused on war, it will halt the progress of the government and the nation. The real crisis of most nations is one of leadership and management.

Good leadership puts the needs and interests of the citizens at the centre of their policies.

As citizens, one major prayer we need to pray for our leaders is that they will have wisdom and the love of God for their people. Every leader requires a great vision, accountability, integrity, strategies etc. We are encouraged to pray for our pastors and leaders in the church community. God would strengthen them and they lead in boldness and accomplish the will of God.

Prayer Points

- Father Lord, thank You for the men and women who serve in positions of leadership in our country, and for their families too (1 Timothy 2:4).

- Lord Jesus, we want You to always remind our leaders why they have been chosen for public service and give them the heart to have the peoples' best interests at heart (John 15:16).

- We pray Lord, give our leaders the wisdom to approach and handle issues well. Reveal Yourself to them and let them experience Your presence always (1 Kings 3:5-6).

- Father, give our leaders the strength to balance their work and other aspects of their lives so that one will not become a threat to the other. Help them live a balanced life just like Paul who was a tent maker and also a preacher of the gospel (Psalms 127:2).

- We pray for fathers to set good leadership abilities in their homes. May the priesthood garment be evidential in their homes. (John 13:34).

- Lord, teach our leaders to love and care for the people. Let love dwell richly in them and may the fear of the Lord always be their watchword (Joel 2:13).

- Abba Father, let Your love reign supreme in the hearts of our leaders. Lord Jesus, help our leaders show a Christ-kind of love to those around them (Colossians 3:14-15).

- We pray Lord, give us leaders who will lead with the fear of the Lord. We ask for leaders who are always after God's will for our nation and not those controlled by selfish ambitions (Nehemiah 5:19).

- Open the eyes of our leaders to understand their roles and duty and help them deploy these effectively (Psalm 119:18).

- Our father may You unite our communities and help us build a better future together. Let love dwell among us (Colossians 3:16).

- Help our leaders make the right decisions at all times. We know that any decision about the nation will affect our economy. Therefore, we ask that the spirit of wisdom rest upon every one of them. (Proverbs 3:5-6)

Prophetic Declarations

- We make a declaration that this nation is for Christ. No demonic law or policy will survive in our nation. This land is Christ's and His kingdom will reign supreme.

- I decree peace all over this nation. By the mercy of the Lord, let an end come to the wars among nations and I decree economic stability all over the nations of the world.

- I call forth the hand of God to rest upon all our leaders and the wisdom of God become evident in their lives.

- I decree that the Lord will raise for Himself in our nation, men like Daniel who have the Spirit and who do the bidding of heaven excellently.

- The Wisdom of God will become evidential in the dealings of our leaders from henceforth.

- We pray the Love of God will spread abroad on the tablets of their hearts. May they rule from a heart of love.

- I declare spiritual sensitivity for all our political leaders in this country. May their eyes of understanding be enlightened to know what the good and perfect will of God is.

- I decree that our leaders will not give up when it matters and they will lead us to safety. The Lord will grant them divine ideas to ensure the safety of the nation.

- Lord Jesus, lead our leaders and let Your Spirit inspire their policies, actions and its implementation.

- Holy Spirit, baptise our leaders with power and wisdom. Let them be guided by the Holy Spirit in every matter.

- I receive mercy for my community in the name of Jesus. Mercy prevails over judgement for us.

PRAYER FOR THE NATIONS

*"If my people, who are called by my name,
will humble themselves and pray and seek
my face and turn from their wicked ways, then
I will hear from heaven, and I will forgive
their sin and will heal their land."*

2 CHRONICLES 7:14

Sometimes, it feels difficult to know what to pray for, especially when it comes to praying for the nations, though you might have some deep pain in your heart and a burning desire to pray. Several global issues are battling many countries of the world.

For example, African nations are ravaged by hunger, poverty, diseases, crime and corruption. Asia, America and Europe are not left out—the war between Ukraine and Russia, climate change worldwide, and terrorism ravaging several other nations are just a few of the global issues the world is battling.

There has never been a better time to pray for your nation. As a believer, you must not feel complacent about your country's current state. God hears when we pray. He hears our cries and knows what we are going through. We can accomplish a lot by turning to God together and praying for our country.

The Church needs to rise to her responsibility of restoring sanctity, tranquility and peace through fervent prayers for the world's nations. We need to rise in the place of prayer, be on guard and keep the night watch till we see the Lord rain mercy upon us again.

Now, you must understand that prayer for your nation is not an option for you as a believer. Even if a crisis hasn't hit your nation yet, you don't have to wait till it does. Nobody expected the shooting and killings in two different schools in America. Whoever thought the Ukraine-Russia war would linger so long, so much so that nations' economies would crumble. What about the lockdown worldwide due to the outbreak of COVID-19? You don't have to wait until the devil takes hold of your nation, state, country and neighborhood before you start praying. This is the best time to vehemently fight him on your knees. Let us pray!

Prayer Points

- We thank You Lord for being the universe's Creator. We know that our nation was founded on Your Word, and we recognise that our progress and growth as a nation can only be possible and sustained by Your Word (Proverbs 16:4).

- We know you are the God of peace. We ask that You speak peace to every troubled nation of the world. Just as You declared peace to the stormy sea and it obeyed (Matthew 8:23-27), speak peace to our nation. Let an end come to war, fighting and killing.

- Awaken us oh Lord! Let us rise in the unity of faith and speak Your counsel upon this land. We pray that You make Your Church speak in unity. We ask, oh Lord, that the Church will rise as one entity to proclaim Your will in this nation till all the good counsel of the Lord about this country comes to fulfilment.

- We command the devil to loose your grip upon this land. In the name of Jesus, we end every demonic activity waging war against the souls of young men and women in this nation, causing them to do unspeakable things. We decree tonight, "Devil, take your hands off our young ones in the name of Jesus."

- We declare healing for this land. As God sent Moses as the prophet of Israel to heal the bitter water of Marah, we ask, Lord, that You heal our Land (Exodus 15:22-25). Please, Lord, make our land yield productively for us and make everything we do in this land prosper.

- We pray the mercy prevails over judgement (James 2:13). Father Lord, let Your mercy prevail over this nation. We know that the blood of the innocent is crying for vengeance, but we ask for mercy, Lord. Show us Your mercy in this land, Lord.

- Dear Lord, I come to You on behalf of our political and religious leaders. The heart of the king is in your hands, and You turn it whichever way You choose (Proverbs 21:1). So, I pray that you direct the heart of our leaders to make choices and decisions according to Your Word. We pray that they will not lead us astray.

- I understand that wars and rumors of war are the signs of the end time. So, Lord, I pray that as we enter the last days, there will be an intense demonstration of Your power. We ask that the spirit of faith be made stronger. Men will rush to God and miracles will become our everyday life's experience.

- We pray father that you allow righteousness prevail in this land. We understand from the Scriptures that righteousness exalts a nation. I pray that men will be convicted of their sins and run to God massively in these last days. I speak in the name of Jesus that the hearts of men will be drawn to God the more.

- I thank You because You always hear me whenever I call You. Thank You because my nation is for You only. Glory to God in the highest!

Prophetic Declarations

- We decree and declare peace over this nation. Let your peace reign supreme in our land. Help us to live peaceful and quiet lives. I pray that You make our leaders advocate for peace and let their mouths be filled with edifying words.

- Upon this land, the Lord will hear our cry for mercy and turn our situation around. I decree that mercy will make the difference in this nation (Psalms 116:1-2).

- I decree under open Heaven that this land will never be a wasteland. The Lord shall exalt the horns of this nation and men will flow into it. In the name of Jesus, we shall no longer be termed "forsaken".

- I decree and declare that the wisdom of God will be evident upon our leaders. May we not be ruled by leaders whose minds are corrupted by the devil. Every one of our leaders in this nation will be men and women after God's heart.

- I agree with God's promises for this nation that in the last days, God's Spirit will be poured out massively upon all flesh. Righteousness and truth will prevail in the land. Men and women all over this nation will serve God passionately. *"For I will pour water on the thirsty land, and streams on the dry ground; I will pour out my Spirit on your offspring, and my blessing on your descendants. They will spring up like grass in a meadow, like poplar trees by flowing streams (Isaiah 44:3-5).*

- I decree and declare that the heart of our leaders in this nation will be kindled with the flame of love and service of humanity. They will serve with their whole hearts.

- I speak and decree that it's time for a shift in this nation. Listen to the Word of the Lord and I decree that you must obey your Maker. This land is known for joy, peace and freedom. Oh ye nation, redemption comes for you henceforth. You are redeemed from wickedness from today.

- I decree supernatural angels of God to be on guard round about our nation. As fire surrounded Jerusalem, so shall the angels of the Lord be on the watch at every corner of this nation. I decree and declare divine protection over every citizen and every person in this nation.

- I destroy every trap of the enemy to ensnare our cities and put the whole nation in bondage. I uproot anything my Heavenly Father has not planted in the hearts of both the young and old of this nation.

- I declare that the Lord reigns over our nation supremely. Our president, senators, representatives, kings and rulers will live peaceable lives with goodness and honesty to do that which is just and right always (1 Timothy 2:1-2).

SALVATION PRAYER

Have you made Jesus your personal Lord and Saviour? If you have not, I urge you to pray this prayer and start a new life with Christ:

> **Dear Father,**
>
> I come to You in the name of Jesus. I admit that I am not living right with You. I know I am a transgressor. But from now on, I want to be right with You. Dear God, I ask You to forgive me of all my sins.
>
> Your Word says that if I confess with my mouth, "Jesus is Lord" and believe in my heart that God raised Him from the dead, I will be saved (Rom. 10:9). I believe with my heart and I confess with my mouth that Jesus is the Lord and Saviour of my life. Thank You for saving me!
>
> In Jesus' name I pray. Amen.

www.ingramcontent.com/pod-product-compliance
Lightning Source LLC
Chambersburg PA
CBHW032003080426
42735CB00007B/501